BEYOND EFFECTIVE

For Josh:

Peace, prosperity, and leadership!

David Perr

DAVID PECK

BEYOND EFFECTIVE
Practices in Self-aware Leadership

Trafford
PUBLISHING™

Order this book online at www.trafford.com/07-2351
or email orders@trafford.com

Most Trafford titles are also available at major online book retailers.

Note for Librarians: A cataloguing record for this book is available from Library
and Archives Canada at www.collectionscanada.ca/amicus/index-e.html

Printed in Victoria, BC, Canada.

ISBN: 978-1-4251-5325-0

*We at Trafford believe that it is the responsibility of us all, as both individuals
and corporations, to make choices that are environmentally and socially sound.
You, in turn, are supporting this responsible conduct each time you purchase a
Trafford book, or make use of our publishing services. To find out how you are
helping, please visit www.trafford.com/responsiblepublishing.html*

*Our mission is to efficiently provide the world's finest, most comprehensive
book publishing service, enabling every author to experience success.
To find out how to publish your book, your way, and have it available
worldwide, visit us online at www.trafford.com/10510*

www.trafford.com

North America & international
toll-free: 1 888 232 4444 (USA & Canada)
phone: 250 383 6864 ♦ fax: 250 383 6804
email: info@trafford.com

The United Kingdom & Europe
phone: +44 (0)1865 722 113 ♦ local rate: 0845 230 9601
facsimile: +44 (0)1865 722 868 ♦ email: info.uk@trafford.com

10 9 8 7 6 5 4 3 2

This book is dedicated to my coach, Dr. Michael Apple-bee, whose guidance, inspiration, spirit, love, and insight has helped me—and many others—discover where heart and work come together. May his higher power keep him with care now that he has departed.

Peace does not mean to be in a place where there is no noise, trouble, or hard work. Peace means to be in the midst of all those things, and still be calm in your heart. That is the real meaning of peace.

—Anonymous

Contents

Introduction

Bookstores and experts are brimming with great advice about effective leadership. And why not? Being effective is a reasonable goal. Once that "effective" box is checked, though, some leaders want to take the next step: "Okay, I'm effective.... Now what?"

In fact, my work as an executive coach has shown that such leaders want more—often much more—than just to be effective.

If you may be looking to take the next step beyond effective, then this book is meant for you. The many one-paragraph practices that follow were designed to help you turn untapped potential into greater fulfillment and sustainable positive results.

Take a moment now to consider what might be different about the way you would lead and operate professionally if you were to go "beyond effective" and work with ever-growing commitment, meaning, and self-awareness. Would things in your world look, sound, and feel different than they do today?

The road to self-awareness is not for the fainthearted, and self-awareness is certainly not a common theme in business books. In fact, as I was working on this project, I began to wonder if leaders and aspiring leaders would even recognize the need for it.

As luck would have it, the answer came during a meeting with the Chief Talent Officer of a well-known

Fortune 500 company. I asked her about a fellow who seemed to many observers to be the obvious potential successor to the company's long-tenured CEO. I wondered how that person was doing in his quest to take over for his boss and run the company. My friend explained that the current CEO had in fact called the man into his office and told him he would *never* be CEO. (The ambitious executive left the company not long thereafter, to "spend more time with the family.") I wondered what the CEO's concern was. She told me: "He said he couldn't let anyone with so little self-awareness take over the company."

So what do I mean by "self-awareness" and "self-aware leadership"? The full meaning is embedded in all of the practices in this book. For discussion purposes, here are six foundational qualities of self-aware leadership:

1. Becoming aware of (and editing) the beliefs that drive our behaviors, actions, and results as a leader

2. Deep humility—curiosity and open-mindedness to ideas, learning, and translating those into systemic change

3. A strong balance between fierce realism and an imaginative vision

4. Timely accountability and responsibility for our impact on others, our community, and on the world overall

5. Leading with great authenticity of heart and mind

6. An unwavering commitment and drive to achieve

These six themes are critical keys to being more than simply an effective leader.

Consider some of the concerns facing today's leader:

acceleration of commerce and the pace of work; widespread geographical neutrality and multiculturalism; rapidly changing technologies; worldwide outsourcing; increasing interdependencies among organizations; performance, legal, market, regulatory, workforce, and governance pressures; and resource challenges. Then throw in family, health, friends, life changes and challenges, community, spiritual life, and heart.

It's clear that the role of the leader today—and even more so tomorrow—is to master speed, turbulence, and complexity. Many leaders manage to cope with these tumultuous conditions, and, as the years click by, to remain in coping mode. Among the successful are those who feel there must be something more—that their best efforts are leaving them exhausted, stressed, and seeking better ways to lead, find greater meaning, or even be happier overall. Sound familiar?

Imagine for a moment that you reset your expectations from simply "coping" to, let's say, *thriving*. Set the bar higher and you'll need to change the way you think about leadership and how you operate day by day. Lasting change always boils down to principles like this: When you replace your core beliefs with ones that serve you rather than work against you, your feelings change, your actions are more powerful, and better results follow.

The hundred practices in this book, a number of which have already appeared in *Business Week Online*, are designed to help you awaken to your own operating system of beliefs, and to do something with what you uncover. That means confronting your blind spots, reassessing outdated standards you have for yourself and others, becoming aware of and learning to manage your negative self-talk at work, and catching yourself when you are getting in your own way or in the way of others. The goal is to help you ride the wave rather than try to remain standing as the next one hits you.

For that, you need to become the world's leading expert on, and to stay in constant touch with, the leader in the mirror. Do this work and, as you lead others, you will model continuous learning and development. That in turn will help your people and your organization to thrive.

During the course of my work as an executive coach, I have seen the following premise proven: The greater your self-awareness, the more of your own potential you will put into action and the more adaptive, skillful, and happy a leader you will be.

Many leaders and aspiring leaders can benefit from these practices. My clients, whether they've been at it for two years or thirty, will usually say something like this:

> *When I became a leader, there was no handbook or road map—I feel like I'm doing it by the seat of my pants. Because I'm the one in charge, people aren't always frank with me. The company's doing well, but other than by looking at the numbers, how do I know I'm doing things the best possible way?*

That's a great starting point—admitting you don't have the answers, may not have all the tools, and are wondering if there's a better way. My work with leaders cannot go forward without such curiosity and humility, two of the most important factors listed above. It's also a great perspective from which to practice the ideas in this book.

Ahead you will find practices, but no magic bullets. Why? In the course of my own work as a leader, literally from mailroom to executive suite and now as a coach, I have been "taking notes" about what works. I've learned that capable, motivated people have their own, best, most fitting answers—better than any canned advice or ancient wisdom I could quote. I developed these practices to help you tap into your own core assumptions about leadership, pick out the less effective ones, and replace them with high-performing beliefs.

The book is organized into five sections of nineteen to twenty-one practices. They are not going to be all-inclusive of what's needed for all leaders, nor will each one be right for you.

There are as many ways to use this book as there are readers like you: For example, open up to a random page each week and take on the practice you find there; use a particular concept as a starting point for a candid discussion or one-on-one with someone who reports to you, or with someone you mentor; ask a trusted advisor or coach for feedback for yourself; write out in journal format your response to a practice and, when ready, move on to another; and so on.

As they say in recovery circles, take what you find useful, and leave the rest. Some of the notions here will hold no resonance for you, others will bother or challenge you (my favorite!), and still others may be reassuring. All of them are intended to provide ongoing support that will offer you the chance to take your full, untapped potential for a new ride on the wave of continuous change.

If you're willing to take a little risk, get bothered, and lean into what you don't know, even if it might "sting," then this book is for you. I hope so, because what you can create is limited only by your beliefs.

1. The Leader's Core

This section focuses on the core traits and tools of self-aware leadership. Think of them not as a list of management skills to be learned and mastered—but rather as ongoing dynamic and evolving practices, each one including a cycle of reflection, acceptance, and change as warranted. After you read each practice, try it on like a new pair of glasses with which to take a fresh look at your beliefs and how they translate into the way you are leading. What do you see that you didn't know before? What do you like and want to keep? What do you think needs to change? Where might you need some help? Stay curious and open-minded to change as you view your world and yourself through each of these lenses.

Leadership from the Heart

Leadership is about the heart. It's been said that every business decision is a personal decision. Leaders who believe that business is separate from heart are missing information that can lead them to their greatest contributions: innovation, inspiration, development of community and opportunities for others, meaningful work, outstanding and ethical governance, and overall success. We appreciate and are inspired by leaders who put their heart fully into their clients, employees, organizations, partners, and communities. Take every opportunity to invite and accept feedback, reflect, learn, and be open to your own feelings. Align your head with your heart in all you do.

The Core of Self-aware Leadership

Self-aware leaders inspire others to do their best work. They generally share six qualities: deliberate and high-performing core beliefs, humility/open-mindedness, balance between realism and vision, authenticity of heart and mind, and an unwavering commitment. Moderation and balance are important, as most of these traits taken too far will tip the scales from asset to liability. It's good to challenge yourself from time to time—reflect on your current situation and see if you are short on one or more of these qualities. What can you do to bring them all into the picture? And if one trait dominates the others, how can you bring about balance? Reflecting on these questions will help you take a major step toward infusing your leadership with the inspiration that will move others to move mountains.

Leadership Signature

The most compelling leaders have developed a unique "leadership signature" that embodies their core values, reflecting these to the outside world. This "signature" includes attentiveness, energy, appearance, presentation/ communication style, and level of poise under pressure. Failing to develop a signature of your own—or using an inauthentic one—diminishes a leader's impact and credibility. How does your signature—what others experience of you in terms of appearance, communication, style, and behavior—enhance or diminish your ability to lead? What do you need to do to synchronize your outward characteristics with your principles? Answering these questions will help you tap into your greatest strengths.

Continuous Learning

Great leadership is fed by continuous learning, which requires an open mind and heart. In this hyperstimulated world of demands and actions, we can't absorb the lessons all around us without quiet time to reflect on and absorb what it is that people, situations, and our results can teach us day after day. Are you engaged in continuous learning and encouraging your people to do the same? Consistently make time to reflect on and incorporate your life lessons, and urge your people to do likewise. Your return on investment will be heartfelt—your continual improvement and theirs.

Enjoyment

When you choose to enjoy your work, you lead with greater power, and change lives for the better. Leaders who make enjoyment a high priority are energized and rewarded by their job, and inspire their people and customers at the same time. Yet thinking it's a "nice to have" and settling for less is so often the norm. Finding enjoyment is often an "inside job"—that is, taking a look at your own beliefs about fun and work, and revising them as necessary to allow for enjoyment. What stands in the way of looking forward to your work most days? It's up to you—it's never too late to remove or change the beliefs or other factors that keep you from enjoying what you do.

Realism

Making a dream come true requires a leader to be realistic about expectations, resources, people, and circumstances; "situational awareness" is the aviation term for it. For leaders, that means having clear standards and milestones with which to chart our course—and reasonable expectations about progress. When we hit the inevitable setback, failure, or unexpected twist, realism asks that we accept, forgive, and change direction accordingly rather than hold onto a regret or to wish or hope that things would be different. Where might a good dose of realism help you implement a better measure or a course correction? The answer to that can help you discover important clues to more-rapid progress.

Accountability

Accountable leaders credit others when things go well, and look to themselves when they don't. Fear-based leaders credit themselves with success while outsourcing failure. All of us have our own way of handling accountability for the consequences of our actions and decisions. True accountability transcends credit or blame; it's about taking the next right actions. Ask yourself how you—and those around you—handle accountability in both positive and negative situations. If you see room for improvement, take the opportunity to make changes that increase your own accountability, and help your team do the same.

Authenticity

The actions of the most compelling leaders have a distinct authenticity of heart and mind that others can appreciate. It's based on how consistently their decisions, communication, and responses to adversity reflect their most heartfelt principles. In their relationships and tasks, authentic leaders are apt to be unguardedly themselves, and not what they think others want or expect them to be. They keep a wary eye in the mirror for any temptation to massage the message, or to ignore their inner compass just to keep the wheels of progress turning. How authentic do you allow yourself to be with others? What holds you back from being more transparent to others? What actions are you willing to take to be true to yourself in the presence of others?

Integrity

Solid integrity in a leader opens an organization's doors to greatness. You can practically feel it in the air (and intuitively know when it's missing)—it fosters loyalty among employees, keen interest among prospective hires, and enables powerful collaborations and deals to be made. Yet we are not machines—at times we get out of sync with our own integrity. To minimize this risk, make it a practice to ask yourself these two questions: *Am I walking my talk most of the time? Am I behaving fairly and honestly without fail, even when times are tough?* Let your responses guide and help you make any necessary adjustments.

Kindness

Aside from having us feel good, self-aware leaders know that genuine kindness creates a competitive advantage. In a world dominated by the tyranny of short-term results, it needs to be recognized as a key factor in success. Take advantage of daily opportunities to be giving of your time and attention to others. Leaders who are generous to customers, community, and investors increase the value of their brand. And when they make the needs of employees a priority, they inspire loyalty and trust—which energizes people to work hard and at peak creativity. The result is a lasting competitive edge that coincidentally happens to feel good, , and coincidentally happens to make the world a better place.

Curiosity

Never-ending curiosity is a core leadership tool. In contrast, the leader who behaves like a perpetual expert shuts people up, and shuts them down. Curiosity involves rejecting the notion that we have (or are expected to have) all the answers, and being vulnerable enough *not* to know. Make it a personal practice to ask questions as would a child or a student in class—and on an ongoing basis. Notice also any important situations or people about which you may *lack* curiosity—that's usually a sign that you are avoiding or missing something important. As you cultivate a sincere curiosity, course corrections for you as a leader, and for your business or projects will present themselves more rapidly, and with sufficient time to implement them. Your people will view you as more approachable, and able to handle whatever they may have to tell you.

Influence

With increasing interdependencies among organizations, governments, and economies, success often rests on a leader's ability to influence those with whom they have little or no positional authority. Consider four components of wielding influence successfully: (1) Emphasize relationships, which endure over time, in equal measure to immediate tasks, which come and go, (2) align mutual interests by understanding what each person is up against and sharing in that vulnerability, (3) incorporate solutions to others' problems within the framework of your needs; and (4) help watch their back for them. Strong relationships enable you to get the job done—and, beyond that, are rewarding at a more heartfelt and human level over time.

Humility

Humility in a leader is necessary to maintain perspective and operate at full potential. Without a bit of humble pie, we can end up wielding power overbearingly, which causes others to react to our arrogance by losing interest in our mission. Even garden-variety arrogance, such as overconfidence, can crop up at times—it's up to each of us to rein it in. Maintain an attitude of gratitude toward your people, schedule an "ego check" with a trusted advisor, and ask yourself how you can be of service to others—these are all useful practices of humility.

Rest

Time off is not a luxury, it's a responsibility of leadership. As the weeks tick by, it's easy to catch ourselves thinking that a vacation would be an indulgence, and/or that our work is too important to leave. But without taking time to recharge, problem-solving abilities actually tend to diminish, and we begin to miss critical, often obvious, opportunities. If it's difficult to remember your last quality time off, that's an indicator that the return on your efforts may be diminishing—perhaps without your awareness. When you regard taking a vacation seriously, you understand that time off is not only about re-connecting with yourself, your family, and your friends—it's a vital opportunity to gain a fresh perspective and a new approach to the work itself.

Task and Relationship

Self-aware leaders balance their time well between tasks and relationships. Overly relationship-centered people can be likable but don't seem to get much done. "Results-or-else" people tend to lose sight of humanity and get obsessed with the goal or project at hand—making colleagues feel they are merely a means to an end. While tasks or projects come and go, never forget that relationships are an enduring source of strength in the workplace. As you focus on results, remember that the strong bonds you create by investing in relationships not only help you achieve these results, they create an environment that fosters loyalty and respect, where colleagues feel valued. By balancing tasks and relationships, you can find the perspectives and resources needed both to achieve success and to weather the inevitable storms along the way.

Delegation

Extraordinary leaders are great delegators. They avoid the three most common impediments to excellent delegation: ambiguous requests, misjudgment of capability or motivation, and reluctance to relinquish sufficient control. They begin by choosing a trustworthy, capable, motivated person. Then, once a clear request is made and agreed upon, they step back and let the process work, verifying progress along the way. When specifically asked for assistance, a good delegator acts as a coach, asking results-oriented questions and listening deeply. Strong delegation will enhance and multiply the resources at your disposal—and you may be happily surprised at what your best people can do when you trust them and offer your support.

Acceptance and Self-will

As leaders, we are often tempted to try to force outcomes, expending enormous energy and force of will for little gain. Acceptance does not mean you agree or approve of certain things—it means you acknowledge them as being exactly the way they are. When we take this step, we replace wishes with reality, making room for new opportunities. Considering your organization and people, what do you need to accept that is unlikely to change? Answer that question and you will find new solutions to continuing problems.

Powerful Inaction

Leaders tend to operate in a constant state of action. In the results-driven workplace, they win by multitasking and by juggling priorities. After enough time living and working this way, the relationship between what we're doing, why we're doing it, and where we're headed can become blurred. When deeper questions like these begin to surface, you need to take a step back and reflect—resisting the urge to *do*. Face the most significant matters with the quiet presence to observe, to feel, and to listen to your heart—and your way forward will become clear. Only then does taking action make sense.

Removing Your Mask

Maturing as a leader involves removing masks that inter-fere with your message. Whether they take the form of a "game face" during tough times, or a "poker face" when confronting uncertainty, well-intended disguises are rampant in the work world. This is particularly common with newer leaders, who often feign confidence when navigating new territory or encountering difficult situ-ations. But hiding from others saps your strength, con-fuses others, and, in the end, can lead to failure. By con-trast, authenticity—thinking, speaking, and being openly committed to your core values in all situations—is key to great leadership. Dare to remove your mask—while at first you may feel overexposed and vulnerable, in the long run you will be happy you did so.

Balance at Work

Authors and experts are very busy telling leaders to find "work/life balance." Yet technology surrounds and links us constantly to a virtual office of unlimited expectations—even further blurring the lines between work and life. How can you create equilibrium day in and day out? For starters, disconnect at some point each day, taking a short time just for you—to clear your mind and focus on something peaceful. A little bit of daily "you time" goes a long way, yielding renewed vigor and clarity.

Peaceful Leadership

It's a common belief that productivity and hard work result from a state of constant motion, tension, and aggressiveness. Exceptional leaders shed this wasteful misconception. Instead, they rely on a sense of peace to achieve sustainable success. Peaceful leaders find extraordinary solutions and practical direction in the calm environment they create for themselves and others. Given this awareness, consider what you can change about yourself, and/or with your organization in order to create a sustainably calm and productive atmosphere.

2. Leading Your People

Your people are your most strategic and valuable asset as a leader, and often your biggest expense. They are also beautifully human: miraculous, mysterious, and even annoying. Given these factors, no one can dispute the need for leaders to awaken and reawaken to their own impact on their people, and to continually improve their own ability to assess, understand, listen, coach, support, and guide others. This is an area where many bad lessons learned earlier in life and career can wreak havoc, and where building self-awareness can literally mean the difference between failure and success, between stress and fulfillment, and, more importantly, between leaving a trail of bodies behind or touching and making a positive difference in the lives of your people. Try on these practices for size, taking from them what helps you and leaving the rest.

A Human Approach

Organizations of all sizes are faced with unprecedented marketplace pressures. Leaders try to get their people to do more, while available resources are diminished in the name of productivity and prudent financial controls. As a result, many places are becoming "burnout organizations" where workers are treated more as office equipment than human beings. To avoid this, leaders need to treat people with humanity and respect, even when they must make difficult choices. Not only does this make sense on a spiritual and ethical level, it creates a workplace that enables you to attract and retain the very best people.

A Culture of Truth

Extraordinary results over time require an environment in which those you lead are *rewarded* for being exceptionally honest. Research has shown such candor to be a priority at companies that sustain outstanding financial results over time. Take a hard look at how you respond to your people when facing their brutal honesty—your responses as a leader weave the culture of your organization. Whatever values you espouse in principle, how frank are you, and how candid are your people with each other—and with you—in actual practice? What do you need to change to build honesty and directness into the DNA of your enterprise?

People Standards

The three most important standards for choosing people are their capability/skills, their self-motivation, and a mutually great fit for them, you, and your needs as an organization. At times, leaders fail to set standards or overlook them—they may instead choose or retain people for more subjectively biased reasons. In such cases, your team, your organization, clients, and even the ill-suited hire tend to suffer. Take this opportunity to develop and/or review your standards for the people you are choosing to include. Then compare each person's attributes against those benchmarks and be open to what you discover—even if it means making some difficult choices.

An Open Mind

Self-aware leaders ask great questions, unencumbered by any need to present themselves as experts. Many—particularly people new to management—wrongly believe that their role is to have the answers and appear authoritative. However, the less you think you know, the likelier you will be to discover creative—and even brilliant—solutions. A leader who understands that ongoing progress requires continuous learning, and that learning begins with an open mind, has a keen advantage over others. Consider the questions: *What are we avoiding here?* and *What is needed for us to remove these barriers?* and *How can we turn this problem into an asset for us?* When you pose challenging questions to your team, enormous resources and enthusiasm are unleashed.

Listening Deeply

How well are we listening to others? The breakneck pace of professional life today keeps us multitasking and, in truth, not listening very well at all. Yet we can gain much-needed perspective on the key puzzles and opportunities before us by pausing and listening deeply to our people, clients, and trusted advisors. Deep listening asks us to value the moment (and the other person) by stopping our mental chatter and taking a pause from the phone, screen, PDA, e-mail or to-do list. Clear your mind and just focus in on the other person as if he or she were the most important person in the world at that moment. That small effort engages your intuition and your heart, tools that work together to turn your interactions into insights.

Believing in Someone

One of the most powerful things we can do as leaders is to show people we believe in them; we always remember those who believed in *us*. When you honestly communicate with conviction about someone's capability or contribution, follow up by acknowledging it, and even present a further opportunity for the person—it can change the course of a day, a project, a life. Even a confident, capable person will be more energized and more likely to thrive with such support. Saying "I believe you can do it, and here's why" is a simple act, yet one with great impact on others—a statement which is neither offered glibly, nor withheld.

Motivation

Leaders who understand what motivates and demotivates their people have a leg up on others. Even so, assumptions can be dangerous—one especially underappreciated aspect of leadership is learning how to discard your bias and ask questions instead. Even if you think you already know the answer, ask the members of your immediate team, one on one, what they find motivating and demotivating. Encourage them to do the same with *their* people. Armed with such information, you are able to make better choices about roles and delegation.

Transmitting or Receiving

As leaders, we often find ourselves more on "transmit" than "receive." Without monitoring the balance between the two, we can become isolated from the news and information that can help us guide our people. Typically, a leader "stuck on transmit" is unaware of it. While some brave person may bring that to your attention, it's really up to you, on a regular basis, to spend some time monitoring your own balance between "transmit" and "receive." Ask yourself questions like *What percentage of that meeting was I talking versus listening?* and *How much of that conference call was I really in a deep listening mode?*

Trust and Control

Excessively controlling behavior—hovering over people and projects—is often confused with leadership. This approach merely exhausts everyone and wastes resources. But how do you know when your good intentions to "help" or "guide" or "coach" have crossed the line? A sign of this might be that your people tend to be compliant, shying away from making bold choices or suggestions. You may also find yourself exhausted, acting more as caregiver than delegator. If your people are capable and motivated, then ask yourself what stands in the way of stepping back and allowing them greater independence. When you demonstrate trust, people feel valued and are inspired to make more-significant contributions on their own.

Reflecting the Best

When individuals who report to you, or a team, hit a low point or find themselves in a prolonged tough situation, notice how it often seems difficult for them to imagine new possibilities. Heavy hearts or drained brains rarely find innovative solutions. You can truly help them by asking questions that offer new vistas, remind them of their capabilities, and open up paths they hadn't considered taking. This literally helps them find their own way from where they are to where they hope to go. We're at our finest as leaders when we help people through a rough patch by showing them where to look for and find their own strength and resources.

Skillful Feedback

Candor among your team is critical for sustainable success—and that starts with the ability to give feedback well. Great feedback is given, first, with the recipient's permission, and it is also timely, private, constructive, candid, and succinct. These elements make it possible for people to hear substance they might otherwise reject, especially if it comes with a clearly defined, clearly communicated suggestion for taking different action in the future. Making a habit of giving feedback this way drastically reduces the chances they will feel "ambushed" at review time. What needs to change, either in yourself or your organization, for you to emphasize and execute highly skillful feedback?

Appreciation

Take the time to notice and appreciate the good work of your people. Showing gratitude feels good, and is a simple yet powerful way to foster strong and sustainable work contributions, and even a little bit goes a long way. It takes only a few moments to give a pat on the back, make a quick phone call, or dash off a note to let someone know she or he did a great job. If you are consistent and sincere and use a personal touch to show your gratitude, you will build a more enjoyable and committed work environment.

Developing Future Leaders

Identifying and grooming potential leaders is critical for organizational continuity at the top. Baby boomers are retiring in massive numbers, and we are facing a potential leadership talent drain of 30 percent or more through 2012. Great organizations get ahead of this curve by getting their leadership—and even outside help—to groom, coach, and mentor potential leaders. Those who don't make such efforts end up settling for the wrong people in key roles, or hiring from the outside—a much riskier venture. What do you need to change to systematically select potential leaders and support their development? A strong program is worth its weight in recruiter's fees.

Whom to Coach

As previously stated, coaching and feedback are important to the future of an organization, through the retention and growth of good people. Yet coaching takes a significant investment of time and energy on the part of an organization and its leadership. Successful coaching can only occur, therefore, with those who are capable, motivated to learn and achieve, and open to being coached. Leaders who attempt to coach people who do not fit this profile are likely to be disappointed.

Coaching Capabilities

When you want to help people achieve more-effective results in a given situation, consider coaching them. Coaching does not need to be complicated or drawn out. It requires only that you ask results-oriented questions, listen deeply, and go with the next question that naturally arises. When you engage in this process long enough, people begin to catch on to their problems and to make new choices on their own. Leaders who coach, and who actively resist the temptation to solve or advise, find that their people develop important new capabilities that can be brought to bear in future situations.

Coaching, Not Telling

Coaching is often confused with giving feedback or telling someone how to do something better, faster, or smarter. "Let me give you some coaching here..." followed by advice, war stories, or feedback, is not coaching. As previously stated, "telling" shuts down people's problem-solving initiative and fosters dependence on you. When you find yourself tempted to "coach" people in this way, then you are acting as teacher or parent rather than mentor or guide. It's easy to confuse giving advice with helping someone, but it's important to remember that your capable, self-motivated people have their own best-fitting answers, even better than anything you can *tell* them.

Assessing Your People

An accurate assessment of your people is a key element of leadership. Personal bias or popular opinions don't lead to sound decisions about deployment or promotion. Instead, review people's actual work using three criteria: *How does the person tend to get in his or her own way? Does the person detect and correct his or her own errors? Do the person's results demonstrate self-motivation and capacity for learning and growth?* Next, ask yourself about "fit": *Where and how will that person deliver his or her best work within your organization?*

Caring

Sustainable leadership requires a strong emphasis on building caring relationships. Connecting deeply with others will foster loyalty—and loyal people do their best work. While managers with more controlling tendencies may succeed for a time, they burn out their stronger, more independent-minded people. As a result, their wins are temporary, lasting only as long as these "leaders" remain the "taskmasters-in-chief." In what ways do you tend to dominate—versus connect with—the individuals on your team? Put your people's well-being on equal footing with your own, and with getting the job done, and you will lead the way to the enduring success of your organization.

3. Guiding Your Organization

There are many conventional notions about guiding an organization to success, and some of those, like "vision" are reflected here. Many others are not, as they are either outside of the conceptual scope of this book, or I felt there were other books and articles that cover them fully. There is one, though, that Jack Taylor, age 80, billionaire, philanthropist, and founder of Enterprise Rent-A-Car, inspired me to include here: *fun*. As Jack explained to me:

> *Just to give you a little background—I was a terrible student in school, and I hated school, and Monday morning was always the worst day of the week for me. I knew the teachers were going to get on me, and I wasn't prepared, and so forth. Then when I got out of the navy, I said, "When I go into business, when Monday morning comes, I'm going to want to feel good about going to work. I want to go to place where I enjoy it and where I look forward to it." And when I started the business that's what I said—I want to get up every morning and go to work and feel good. I want the people to be happy. I want the customers to be happy, and I want to be happy. And I think we've basically succeeded with that.*

As you try on the practices in the section, ask yourself how the concept of enjoyment at work underlies everything, and what needs to change for that to happen for you and your people. You'll be glad you started that particular line of reflection!

Vision

What would a future far greater than the present look like for you? A thorough grasp of that target is critical to leadership—it provides a beacon for all to follow, and to help you refocus when you get off track. Get your vision clear in your heart and communicate it, together with your intentions and concerns, to your people. Aim high, select the right team, work diligently, make sure you are true to yourself and your values along the way, and, equally important, have faith. It may be both difficult and rewarding—and also much better than you envisioned.

Detach from Outcomes

Leadership often means riding a curveball—so it helps immensely to be flexible about the exact form your desired vision or goal will take. Indeed, leaders who are overly rigid about precise outcomes create their own difficulty when dealing with turbulence or change. A certain degree of detachment from outcomes allows you to be awake to change in real time, and alter course as needed. Paint your vision of the future, and then detach from the exact way it will materialize. When you operate from anticipation and intention, rather than expectation, you multiply the chances your dream will be realized.

Numbers-based "Leadership"

Solid financial management is essential for any success-ful organization. But when numbers dominate decision making, the trivial can become significant, while growth and innovation tend to stop. By overemphasizing quarterly financial results, an enterprise can literally ravage itself over time. Extraordinary leaders put first their responsibilities to their vision, clients, and then to their employees and the communities they serve, and balance them with good financial management.

Culture: Unspoken Rules

Leaders establish the culture of an organization according to their own actions, as observed by others. In turn, that culture strongly influences how seamlessly things get done. If, for example, you as a leader say, "I call them as I see them," but tend to soft-pedal your own communications, your organization's culture will reflect your *actions*, rather than what you *say*. Similarly, an explicitly values-driven culture provides a shared understanding that enables the individuals in the organization to attain ambitious goals. In what ways does the culture of your enterprise help or hinder the organization's ability to succeed?

Community

The members of a true community share the vision "I will watch out for you." Leaders who take responsibility for participating in a significant way in their community enrich their prospects over the long haul. Yet in the rapid march to their goals, it's easy to overlook or put off until tomorrow the needs of the people and issues just beyond their front door. Take time to define what you consider to be your own community, and then do for it what is needed. When you make it your mission to support the success of your community, it will respond in kind to you and your organization.

Fun

To leaders expecting the absolute best from their people, fun on the job isn't a frivolity, it's a necessity. Leaders who believe work can't or shouldn't be enjoyable create a culture of indifference and stress. Who wants that day in and day out? When playfulness is encouraged, not only do people look forward to coming to work, but new energy and enthusiasm are unleashed on old problems. In fact, organizations that encourage high spirits tend to produce a stronger bottom line. See if your own beliefs or assumptions are standing in the way of an enjoyable atmosphere. Why bother to do this? Everyone, including you, will operate at a peak level when they can have a good time at work.

Being Clear Up Front

Unspoken assumptions about the future are the seeds of disappointing outcomes. Great leaders define right up front the specific results that will not just satisfy but will feel like an absolute home run. Trading off clarity with assumptions, or vowing to figure it out along the way, is too often the norm, done "in the interest of time." It's important to ask yourself which projects or aspects of your organization are losing (or have lost) clarity about where they are heading. Which new initiatives need some bright target to be painted? Some well-placed fleshing out of what "Point B" looks like greatly increases the odds that you and your team will align actual results with your highest-priority goals.

Meaningful Measures

What gets measured improves. Listening to your instincts and intuition is fundamental to great leadership—but only in tandem with clear standards for people and results, and a handful of powerful quantitative indicators of progress. Key criteria for such measures include ease of use, comprehensiveness, and relevance to the desired results. Make it a practice to periodically reassess your benchmarks. Are they easy to understand? Do they locate you precisely, like GPS, in relation to your goals? Do they light up both barriers and drivers to success? Given your answers, what can you do to make them more powerful?

When to Manage

Leaders guide people, resources and strategies toward their vision of tomorrow. Managers focus on the practical realities of today. At times a leader must act as a manager, and it's vital to have standards that tell you when such a time has come—and when it has passed. Without specific guidelines, you risk either being too hands-on, or too hands-off. Given your leadership style and your organization's challenges, what clear signals or measurements would tell you it's time to act as a manager?

Consequences

Setting clear consequences—for success *and* failure—whether you create them, or coauthor them with your people, is an essential responsibility for leaders. Doing so creates the right conditions for peak performance. Recurring mistakes, missed targets, and sustained average performance are all signs of ineffective or missing consequences. What needs to change to establish and apply well-designed consequences for your organization's high-priority goals? Clear consequences create a rewarding environment for those who work hard and stay focused, and help reduce the number of people "weighing down" an organization.

Courage

It takes strength for leaders to take action when they encounter stagnant performance in their organizations. Those who act with deliberateness get far better results than those who resort to delay or avoidance. What gets in the way of taking necessary steps? Most often, fear—of conflict, of having to replace someone, of being perceived as "not nice." Failure to make timely and appropriate decisions undermines both organizational effectiveness, and top performers' respect for management. Dismissing or relocating a consistently low-performing individual, particularly one who is popular or likable, or has been around for a long time, can make unexpected sense not only for the organization but for the person in question.

Measuring Success

Beyond measuring progress in a meaningful way, it's critical to have a truly great measure of economic success—one that will be both concise and memorable, integrating the goals you are striving to achieve. Most important, it needs to reveal to your people whether overall they are moving closer to—or further from—your vision. Design and implement a simple yet profound success measurement for your enterprise. Does it reflect a confluence of passion, economics, and capability? Once it has been formulated, communicate it to your people "in draft" and ask them to help you hone it into something memorable and meaningful. Finally, be open to re-evaluating it from time to time as conditions change.

Failure Standard

Leaders typically work hard to achieve a successful outcome, and recognize it when it happens. Yet it's also critical to set up a standard for when to stop investing in someone or something. Lacking such a "failure standard," we are informed mainly by opinions and hopes. These can lead us to make choices that drain vital resources for too long. Take some time this week to consider your people and projects: Do you have measurable endpoints for both positive and negative outcomes? Challenge yourself to recognize when enough is enough, however difficult it may be at first.

Owning the Solution

Is your team or organization operating at a level you would call "great?" If not, you may have concluded that your people just don't get it or have gone off track somewhere along the way. While one or both conclusions may be true, the first—and sometimes the most important—place to look is in the mirror. Are you providing clear guidance and delegating without hovering? Would your people say they can be candid with you, that they feel heard? While the answers may initially be disturbing, you can usually correct any situation you have created, once you take responsibility for seeking out the solution.

Willingness to Be Wrong

A key component of leadership is the willingness to be wrong. Great leaders use their own potential for error to help them listen with an open mind, really hearing the perspective and ideas of other people. They understand that investing too much in the need to be "right" silences the feedback of others, causing them to shut up and shut down. In fact, the more you are willing to be wrong, the more likely you are to get it right.

Celebration

When was the last time you celebrated something meaningful? Community acknowledgment is a powerful tonic:
People who celebrate milestones tend to have more suc-
cesses to celebrate. Many leaders lose sight of this, as they
focus more attention on what *isn't* working. Celebration
can seem indulgent. Within reason, recognizing suc-
cesses helps motivated people stay that way. It provides
the heartfelt acknowledgment that everyone appreciates.
Which particular milestones or accomplishments, large
or small, are overdue for a celebration in your world?

Results-oriented Questions

How powerful are the questions you ask? When it comes to getting things done, "why" questions invite others to explain or justify the past, keeping things in problem mode. "What" and "how," though, focus attention on the present and future, where leadership works wonders. As neurolinguistic programming experts Joseph O'Connor and John Seymour point out, "*How* questions will get you an understanding of the structure of a problem. *Why* questions are likely to get you justifications and reasons without changing anything." As a researcher, it's important to ask why. As a leader, though, it's critical to evaluate the usefulness of the questions you and those around you tend to ask, and modify your approach until find yourself getting the results you intend.

Words and Actions

Leaders inspire loyalty and integrity among others when their actions match their words. Without such congruence, they encounter skepticism and distrust which interfere with an organization's overall morale and ability to achieve. This can in turn reduce the attraction and retention of top talent. While it is unreasonable to expect perfect congruence between words and actions one hundred percent of the time, it is important to recognize when you need to make significant changes in order better to "walk your talk."

Trust and the Team

A team committed to achieving a common goal produces great results when its members trust each other. Without trust, the power of a team is minimized, making it nothing more than a well-intentioned group of individuals. Exceptional teams make trust a deliberate goal and confront real issues and priorities without the need to be reserved, polite, or careful. Everyone expresses the truth about what's important, heartfelt, and at times uncomfortable. Whether you are leading or are a member of a team, it's important to ask yourself and others, *what is the level of trust here?*

Good Intentions

Even the most self-aware leaders get in their own way when good intentions are taken too far. Expansion plans can result in uncontrolled growth; desire for consensus devolves into "analysis paralysis"; a benevolent approach can turn into confusion and accountability issues. These consequences emerge over time and require the leader's attention to address and resolve them. When a goal is elusive, ask yourself: *How are we getting in our own way, and which well-intended behaviors have we taken too far, stretching them into liabilities?*

Gratitude

While it is not the same for everyone, being grateful is a key factor in organizational success. Leaders who promote gratefulness give their firms an edge in the current results-or-else environment. Starting with themselves and including their people, they can ask: "What would need to change for us all to be operating with more gratitude here?" They are then able to make choices that lead to greater meaning for individuals and the organization overall. Recognizing the importance of a grateful heart creates both better short-term results and an enterprise that can sustain superior outcomes well into the future.

4. Turning Challenges into Wins

Many organizations recode the word "problem" into "challenge," and people poke fun at that as a convenient dodge. That said, issues and problems, when framed constructively, are indeed challenges—and such is the breakfast of champions. In addition to learning from self-reflection and from trusted advisors, self-aware leaders learn from the losses, fumbles, setbacks, failures, conflicts, dramas, and catastrophes. These are, after all, universal. We all encounter them more than once, as long as we stretch ourselves beyond just "playing it safe." From such strife we learn much richer lessons than we could gather from hundreds of happy days strung together. That's not to negate the feelings—because denying the feelings that go along with such lessons—fear, shame, anger, frustration, sadness—gives them permanent residency as lumps under the rug of our consciousness, waiting there, where we can trip over them again. Self-awareness challenges us to experience something fully, feel it in detail, and then let it go, and move beyond it, lesson in hand.

What's Needed

When facing a problem—whether a daily annoyance or all-out crisis—a crucial question is, *what's needed here?* Without such orientation, the ego or fear can lead us into the "why" of the unchangeable past, or the "blame/ avoid blame" syndrome. While seemingly innocuous, this question helps leaders avoid reactively wasting time and energy and allows them to take in the whole picture. When you get that hot, stressed-out flush—or the sinking feeling of failure—make it a practice to catch and assess such responses in the moment. Take a breath... and pause. Then ask yourself *what's needed here?* to shift your focus from reaction toward what your team and organization truly require.

Finding Opportunity in Uncertainty

Leaders who regard uncertainty as an opportunity give themselves a boost. Significant time and effort are often wasted by those who want to convince themselves or others they have The Answer. But "I know" or "I'm certain" closes the door to new insight and learning—both so critical to dynamic organizations. Conversely, "I don't know" allows for discovery, innovation, improvements, and achievement. In fact, the more you admit you don't know, the more you and your people will find novel ways to succeed. Relieve yourself of the pretense of certainty, grab that freedom, and take it for a test drive. Where will it lead? No one knows for sure, but you're likely to tap into answers that would otherwise remain hidden and inaccessible.

Deriving Progress from Failure

Learning from failure—rather than burying it—can fundamentally improve an organization and enhance leadership. Negative outcomes can knock the wind out of the most motivated, capable leader. So it is tempting to sweep the facts or feelings into a dark corner in order to find peace and move on. Yet denial of the lesson leads eventually to a repetition of similar conditions. Face your failure without judging—accept it—own your part of it—and forgive yourself. Doing so clears the way for you to learn from the situation and move on. By helping you connect more empathetically with others facing challenges of their own, failure can enrich your leadership.

Facing Facts

As humans, we are all prone to avoidance and even denial from time to time—leaders are no exception. Take a fresh look at any long-lasting, difficult situation, and you are likely to find some level of your own denial which is prolonging or even aggravating the problem. Today is always a good day to seek out what you have been ignoring and to help those you lead do the same. Do this not because it is easy, but because it works. In fact, when you acknowledge a situation as it is, new possibilities emerge. Such acceptance—along with the courage to set a new course from lessons learned—allow us to overcome even the most daunting challenges.

Tough Topics

Once an issue has been faced, it's time to address it. Despite the apprehension we may feel, we know that only good can come from an honest encounter with an issue that won't disappear on its own. The self-aware leader sees a learning opportunity when "tough topics" must be addressed. This means a commitment to direct a good-faith discourse with the sole purpose of resolving whatever is creating problems for you or your organization. Consider the high-priority issues you need to address. Setting the stage for those conversations, ask yourself how you can hold yourself and others to standards of directness, heart, honesty, and freedom from blame. Then simply go ahead and put them on the table.

Anger

Leaders inspire others by being emotionally honest and authentic. So when your temper flares, or resentment builds over time, it's important to find a skillful response to your anger. Whether you bury it or unleash it inappropriately, a misdirected temper can undermine key relationships or team efforts. Instead, exercise restraint of word and action: Take a step back—which, depending on the situation, may mean a momentary pause, or a lengthier time out—to assess the cause. If you are angry mainly because your ego feels threatened, or you're frustrated / disappointed with *yourself*, then work it out on your own, or with a trusted advisor. If, however, your values or standards were overrun by the other person, then, by all means, express yourself to them... after the storm, the air is likely to be clearer for all involved.

Avoidance and Sugar Coating

Sometimes delivering criticism or bad news is a necessity. We do neither our people nor our organization any favors by trying to sugarcoat a direct message. The temptation to avoid conflict, people-please, be liked, or second-guess others' perceptions can lead to tailoring what *must* be said to what it seems others can handle. That can produce confusion. In contrast, when you are direct, respectful, and forward looking with tough messages, the pressing issues and solutions become clearer to everyone—your people will know precisely where they stand and what needs to be done.

Tuning Up Unproductive Conversations

A signal characteristic of unproductive conversations is a focus on the past. Such meetings or discussions lack attention on the present, and even more important, the future. The next time you find yourself in—or are presiding over—a go-nowhere discussion, notice the number of statements people are making about the past. Then break the pattern. Move things into the future with a simple statement like "Let's look at where we are now, and where we need to headed." By doing so, you can turn it into a frank discussion about how to get from where you are to where you want to be. With that simple shift, you will put the conversation on the path to positive results.

Bridging the Candor Gap

A "candor gap" is quite common in organizational set-
tings. Fear of conflict or embarrassment—being wrong
or unpopular—are among the reasons people get in the
habit of being less than candid with each other. People
work at their best when they know where they stand with
you, and with their peers. Each of us is in a position to help
others gain the courage necessary to be direct and honest.
Leaders make it easier for their people to be plainspoken
and bold when they lead by example. Making seemingly
modest investments in your own honesty and managerial
courage will empower others to overcome their fear in a
similar way.

Unproductive Worry

Many leaders committed to success are unaware of the longer-term worries they carry every day. Some believe them to be motivating and tend to operate from a constant state of anxiety. While it's true that adrenalin raises attention and speeds up thinking, on a sustained basis the cost is too high. Worries held over time weigh down leaders and those they lead, impairing efforts. Act on or release a fear and you free up capacity to be creative and productive. Make a practice of assessing the long-term worries that occupy you and addressing them.

Changing Your Mind

Research shows that your beliefs are the foundation for your results: Beliefs determine feelings, both of which lead to actions, which then get results. Positive and constructive core beliefs, therefore, are much better over time than negative ones. Negative beliefs and/or feelings are human, and not to be ignored, but when you're ready to turn a losing situation into something positive, it's helpful to take responsibility for your core beliefs that are running the show. Let the negative feelings and thoughts drain away and then choose a more positive mental approach—for example, a puzzle or game framework. By shifting your perspective from "same old grind" to "puzzle," you unleash curiosity, fascination, possibilities, and, in the end, new outcomes.

Perfection and Procrastination

Many leaders hold themselves and others to high standards. Ambitious goals are great, but taking such standards too far results in perfectionism, an unrealistic or obsessive striving for ideals. Because achieving according to extreme standards of perfection is highly improbable at best, such expectations can actually hinder or stop progress. Since most of us can't meet or even hope to approach perfection, paralysis can set in—we just give up trying. Without understanding the perfection/procrastination cycle, inaction can erroneously appear to be laziness. If you or someone you are leading is procrastinating about something important, look beneath the surface for some brand of perfectionism, double-check your standards, and make the necessary adjustments.

"At Stake" Analysis

At times, leaders will notice a recurring pattern of "underwhelming results." That may mean there is some kind of below-the-surface attachment to the status quo. Asking *Why does this keep happening?* leads only to the identification of symptoms—not root causes. Instead, try asking, *What's at stake if I keep things the way they are?* Take the answer you get, and ask again: *Okay, now what's at stake?* Repeat the question until you can go no further and you are likely to discover the source of the persistent problem. Solutions will then become evident, helping you make whatever changes are necessary to break the pattern.

Productive Disagreement

Disagreement can promote—or hinder—progress and innovation. When the manner of disagreeing lacks the parties' mutual respect and shared responsibility for a solution, paralysis and division fill the void. Leaders need continually to pose the question *What do I need to change so that disagreement unites—rather than divides—the team and the overall effort?* Those who embrace this challenge will be rewarded with innovative results and enduring collaborations with others.

Conflict-friendly Leadership

Leaders who support constructive conflict create an environment that fosters innovation. A culture that is too friendly—one that goes overboard on building consensus and feeling good together—can be symptomatic of deeper issues. You could inadvertently be avoiding candor; garbling otherwise meaningful communication; and hindering teamwork. But as leader you can set the tone, giving your people "permission" for vigorous debate by promoting frank and open discussion. Reasonable disagreement followed by resolution tends to yield rich and productive results. Take a hard look at how you view conflict and how that influences others in your workplace. A conflict-friendly perspective increases your capacity as a leader and enriches the contributions of your people.

Shifting Your Viewpoint

When seriously at odds with someone's point of view, it's important to give ego a few minutes off and reassess the situation from their side of the table. Seeing a situation through the eyes of another and learning what she or he is up against can replace frustration with healthy debate. In fact, by detaching from your own argument, more-insightful decisions can be made. When considering a tough issue, ask yourself what it would take to imagine the view from the other side of the table, then try it.

Balanced Solutions

A strategic partnership or professional relationship can, at times, become imbalanced or unproductive. It can be tempting to put your self-interest first, or to place the needs of the other party ahead of your own, in order to find a quick fix. Both are equally unlikely to produce sustainably favorable results. Ask instead: What solutions will honor the aims and needs of both parties—yours and theirs—equally? Even if current conditions make it seem like a long shot, finding such a balance is always possible with tenacity and hard work. When you forge solutions that work for all parties, including you, you are rewarded with productive relationships that stand the test of time.

Assessing Capacity for Change

As leaders, accurately evaluating capacity for change is as important as any other responsibility we have. Leadership demands that we be unflinching in facing circumstances as they are, making clear choices in any situation. It requires us to live not in the wish or the hope, but in more-grounded positivity. Are we realistic in our expectations? Or are we standing before the orange tree, wishing it will one day yield apples? Checking in with yourself about a person or situation you hope will change reveals new options and choices, grounding you firmly in the present.

Too Much Information

The true cost of overcommunication surprises even the most experienced leaders. Most people in positions of leadership average well over 20 percent of their time creating and/or taking in communication not directly used in achieving their vision. Many update e-mails, conference calls, meetings, PowerPoint reviews, offsite meetings, and other forms of "information sharing" are well-intended wastes of time. Explore how much time your organization spends on unnecessary communication, and set new standards for your team.

Refreshing Your Perspective

E-mails, voicemails, meetings, deadlines, and the un-expected keep us in perpetual motion. As we maintain this pace over time, it's only natural that it takes more effort to be creative and come up with new ideas. A fresh perspective is required for leaders to guide others in new directions. Make it a point to find ways to refresh your viewpoint by taking pauses from the heat of the action—try out a different form of physical exercise, listen to music, engage in a hobby, read, meditate, journal, or take walks. Whatever you choose, make sure you can lose track of time when you do it. Such "timeless" practices are a healthy way to generate new ideas and answers and be a more awake leader.

5. Self-awareness in Practice

How do we incorporate practices specifically designed for greater self-awareness into the throes of daily leadership responsibilities? For the answer, I turned to two things: on the one hand, my empirical leadership experience, and that of my clients and, on the other, principles of 12-step recovery. Why? Just as the recovering addict tackles his or her complex and turbulent behavioral issues, a self-aware leader must tackle the complexity and turbulence of his or her own lower-performing beliefs. By definition, recovery principles are meant to work when they are applied with rigorous honesty and discipline in the all-weather craziness of the real world. My work has shown great synergy between recovery and leadership—those who are serious about recovering from addiction must hold themselves to higher standards, just as leaders, with their responsibilities to others, are invited to set a higher bar for themselves and their people if they want to raise their game. Whether or not recovery has any resonance for you, the practices in this section are designed for leaders committed to self-awareness and going "beyond effective."

Heart as Leadership Compass

The goal of being fit of body and mind is nothing new, but what does it mean to be "fit of heart"? Whenever you are quiet and reflective enough to tap into what's in your heart, it becomes your compass. It points to everything of significance to you as a leader and a person, now and down the road ahead. Sustainable leadership of others is very much about your ability to inspire them—and, in the end, inspiration comes from only one place: the heart.

Feelings and Facts

Great leaders know that a deeply personal investment is needed to guide others to phenomenal results. Operating in balance between both facts and feelings, they are able to inspire others to do their best work. So check in with yourself regularly, assessing how you truly feel, especially when facing challenging questions or problems. Then allow both feelings and facts to work together. In doing so, you will discover your own connection between heartfelt candor and a greater ability to foster the support of others.

Meaning

As leaders, we know the results we want and excellent ways to achieve them. Yet, do we remember, or are we even conscious of, the personal meaning behind our work—what brings us fulfillment in the effort? When we forget to pause and ask ourselves, *For the sake of what am I doing this?*—we can find ourselves complacent; doing work that lacks a sense of meaningful purpose, simply because we haven't asked ourselves about it for too long. Typically, life has an uncanny way of confronting us with this key query, usually at the most inconvenient moments. Why wait?

Purpose

We do our best and are happiest when we seek out and understand our own professional "sweet spot"—where our talent, capabilities, passion, and sense of life purpose meet. It sounds lofty, but is actually pragmatic: Leader A thrives when tackling the thorniest problem around, while Leader B prefers simply to "leave things better than I found them." Make a list of every conceivable fun, engaging work and life experience you can remember. Show this list to a trusted advisor and ask: *What are the common threads?* Once you identify your sweet spot, make the changes that need to be made to align or re-align yourself in a more deliberate direction.

Imagination

Imagination is part of the DNA of leadership. We all have it, whether we know it or not, and everything we do and produce—absolutely everything—is better when fueled by imagination. The world of getting things done and achieving results at all costs would have us believe imagination is for daydreams, weekends, management retreats, or the lucky few who get to use it regularly in their type of work. Yet all creativity springs from it, as we can create only what we can imagine. May your reach exceed your grasp at least once a day—remember that a leader's imagination is a bright spark that illuminates the road ahead for everyone.

Intuition

Research has shown that conscious thought is quite limited in comparison to the much more skillful "non-conscious" mind. The product of this high capacity unconscious "computer" is what we call intuition. Because intuition seems intangible, some find it difficult to trust. Yet when we clear our mind of thoughts and other distractions, we can access this valuable source of insight and solutions. Those who have learned to trust their intuition find it an informative guide to making good choices and taking action. Find a way to clear your mind and to listen to your intuition regularly, whether you are in the shower, the office, or the boardroom.

Vulnerability

It may come as a surprise to some that the greatest human and business collaborations are based on shared vulnerability. Opening your mind and heart to others enables you to match your challenges and ambitions with theirs and to find common ground of great possibilities. If you keep yourself guarded others will respond in kind—which hinders all but superficial success. Leadership requires the courage to make yourself vulnerable to others you want to inspire or guide and to anyone with whom you intend to create anything of lasting value.

Daily Inventory

A very brief, daily self-reflection is a great way to achieve continuous improvement as a leader. Carve out a quiet moment at the end of the day to ask yourself four questions: *How do my actions line up with my principles? Are my efforts helping my people make strong progress toward my vision? How do I feel in my heart?* and, most important, *What do I need to do differently tomorrow?* Taking regular timeouts to notice how you do what you do is a powerful way to keep improving your results.

Blind Spots

A blind spot is everything we can't see about ourselves yet which is obvious to others. It's important to make an ongoing practice of discerning and illuminating your own blind spot, because it can interfere with what you are hoping to achieve, and damage your credibility. Ask those you trust to point out what negative traits you don't notice about yourself, but that impact your work and/or your leadership. While what you learn will likely be embarrassing—especially because although it's new to you, you recognize that it's old news to others—bear with it. The clarity you can gain from illuminating traits that accumulate in your blind spot will mark a giant step forward for you as a person and a leader.

Having Strong Feelings Point the Way

Strong negative feelings are like flags waving over opportunities to become more self-aware, and thereby lead with greater strength. It's natural to look at external events or issues as the source of our discomfort—yet feelings always stem from our *own* thinking. Scratch the surface of your anger, fear, or sadness and you will find underlying principles, assumptions, violated standards, or expectations well worth a closer look. Hold up those beliefs to the light of day with an open mind and heart, and they can help you find a new direction or solution. Revitalized energy and leadership are found by facing and dealing with beliefs head on.

Cleaning Up Negative Beliefs

Beliefs—whether positive or negative—lead directly to feelings, actions, and results. Leaders have a responsibility to heed that "chain of command" and be purposeful and conscious of their root beliefs. While realism is always important, persistent negative thinking tends to yield adverse outcomes. Why? Such negativity gets fed into your nonconscious mind, the "big computer," which then limits your ability to problem-solve, imagine possibilities, perceive, and lead. Organizationally, negative beliefs reinforce naysayers and those who cling to the status quo. Recognizing and "firing" the committee of doubters in your own head is fundamental to achieving both self-aware leadership and sustainable growth.

Knowing Your Gremlins

"Gremlin" is a shorthand term for inner critic, self-doubt, or negative or undermining beliefs, whose power to undermine you depends on their stealth. With practice you can identify and neutralize them by bringing any counterproductive self-talk into the light of your awareness. For a period of time, try listening for the negative things you may be telling yourself and make a few notes about the specifics. Over time you will become more familiar with your gremlins and can learn to manage them from a leadership position.

Rushing to Judgment

Trusting instincts and making rapid choices can help a leader get the job done. Yet when decisiveness is taken too far, we can get in the habit of making choices too quickly, even when circumstances warrant a more nuanced view. Sometimes a closer look is needed to avoid poorly informed decisions and ineffective solutions that can result in unwanted consequences. When you are tempted to "fire" before aiming carefully, take a moment to reflect on all the options open to you. Taking this pause regularly will help you distinguish between rapid decisions and rash ones.

Inertia versus Value

Tasks and relationships that start out requiring reasonable efforts sometimes become struggles. Because this change from productive to strained can happen gradually, it's difficult to notice the tipping point, when the task or relationship is defined more by inertia than by true value for all involved. If something becomes a net drain on your energy, ask yourself: *What do I need to start, stop, change, and/or continue to realign this task or relationship with my vision?* Make a practice of evaluating—or getting help to evaluate—your professional activities, projects, and working relationships. Face facts about anything that has turned into a struggle, and address it.

People Pleasing

Our desire to be liked and loved is primary. Sometimes we translate that into the need to please or caretake others at our own expense, or that of the organization. This need can unintentionally cause more harm than good, particularly if it manifests as a pattern of behavior. Taking too much responsibility for others impairs a leader's ability to make incisive decisions. While kindness is a leadership asset, it needs to be balanced with the greater good, which also includes your own needs and those of the enterprise. As you consider your professional relationships, ask yourself if your concern for others is interfering with your own effectiveness.

Leading and Ego

Self-aware leaders recognize the destructive impact of an unchecked ego. It's easy for the ego to go too far—often outside of our awareness. Grandiosity, narcissism, martyrdom, impatience, and presumption of entitlement are specific signs that our ego is working overtime. Skillful leaders keep a vigilant eye on their ego and aren't afraid to admit a goof or "oops" when it happens. Learning to detect your ego warning signs will enable you to remind yourself to step back, reflect, and give your ego the rest of the day off.

Grounded Positivity

A positive outlook is an effective leadership tool, but only when grounded in reality. When it's taken too far, ungrounded confidence strains credibility and can go on to wreak havoc on budgets, deadlines, and people's commitment to your goals. Yet when that favorable view is balanced with facing facts, assessing weaknesses and vulnerabilities, and making adjustments, then it can indeed inspire your best work and that of others. It's important to know in your heart that you can achieve your vision from the effort and resources you dedicate to it. Trusting that your dreams can come true works best when such confidence goes hand in hand with your own critical, and skillful, vigilance.

Trusted Advisors

It's important for leaders to trust advisors to help them explore new ideas and discover critical solutions. The candor, talents, expertise, and heart of those we choose will help us navigate the road ahead and help illuminate our blind spots. Indeed, leaders without an advisor operate somewhat in the dark, lacking healthy, outside perspective. Like a beacon cutting through the many agendas and ambitions that demand our attention, a trusted advisor has our best interests at heart. What do you need to do to identify and engage in conversation with a trusted advisor regularly?

Coasting

Even experienced leaders find themselves coasting some-times—meeting demands without making significant progress. At such times, ask yourself if you are enjoying a healthy breather—or an unwanted pattern of inaction. When it's the latter, consider the possibility that you may, without realizing it, be gaining something simply by maintaining the status quo—even if it's just the comfort of familiarity. Equally, it's important to notice when you may be unwittingly resisting change. This awareness can help you break through your current bastion of comfort, taking you and your organization to the next level.

Achieving

What it means "to achieve" is unique to each leader. It's healthy to reflect on this from time to time, and consciously choose what it means to you. Otherwise, you can find yourself heading for goals that lack deeper meaning, as if by default, or on autopilot. Take a fresh and honest look at how you define success today—without judging whatever you may discover—and confirm or reset your direction accordingly. Tuning in to your values, and how they shape your idea of success, will help you define and achieve a wholehearted future.

Minding the Future You

It's easy to overlook our own personal growth while leading others to achieve challenging goals. Yet to sustain us
and realize our potential, we must engage in self-develop-
ment. Given the day-to-day demands of leadership, how
do we do that? Start by imagining a future version of
yourself standing at the intersection of your capabilities,
your heart's desire, and your financial goals. Ask yourself
if your current track is moving you toward, or away from
that "future you," and then make adjustments as necessary. You'll be glad you did.

Index

T
Talent Management Magazine • 123
Tasks • 22, 109
Taylor, Jack • 49, 123
Team • 14, 32, 33, 36, 39, 40, 47, 51, 57, 64, 69, 74, 87, 88

U
Uncertainty • 26, 75
Unconscious • 101

V
Values • 10, 26, 31, 51, 54, 115
Vision • 49, 51, 53, 55, 59, 62, 92, 98, 103, 109, 112
Vulnerability •18, 19, 26, 102, 112

W
Washington Post • 123

Acknowledgements

All my love and gratitude to Larry Crevin, David Caploe, Ph.D., and Ray Kelly. Each contributed his smarts and heart to every practice in this book, mostly on Sundays. Special thanks to my editor Anne Ross, and to the team at Trafford.

Very special thanks to all of my clients past and present.

Many thanks to Ken Stram for putting up with me and guiding me. Thanks to Dave Mathews the web wizard, and to Rusty Fischer for telling me to do it myself, and for his advice and counsel. Thanks to Josh Burek at the Monitor; the editors at BusinessWeek Online, the Washington Post, Human Resources Executive magazine, Talent Management magazine, the Journal of Employment Relations, Recognize Service Excellence, American Management Association Online; and the others brave enough to publish my articles and ideas about leadership. Thanks to literary agent William Brown for suggesting I blog, and to my readers at The Recovering Leader.

Very special thanks to Karen Warner at Wiley/Jossey-Bass, who saw my business card and said I should write a book. Thanks also to Neal Maillet for his guidance. Thanks to Jack Taylor, billionaire and philanthropist, who connected the dots for me between leadership and fun. Thank to Suzanne Tucker for telling me to write short leadership messages in the first place.

Deepest thanks to my mentors and coaches: Jane Mc-

Nally, who helped me to choose life, then showed me how; to Michael Bader; Susan Badger; Allen Burke, my loving laser-beam; Michael Applebee, whose loss still stings; the magnificent Barbara Braham; the shining Chris Wahl; Frank Ball; and Lloyd Raines. Thanks to Georgetown Leadership Coaching and its outstanding faculty for embracing the "full catastrophe" of my beginnerhood. Thanks to Enrique Zaldivar for his caring support, and to him and his family for making the world a better place.

Thanks to Marshall Goldsmith, Kathy Gallo, Laura Daley, and Damien Faughnan of Marshall Goldsmith Partners, and to Kathy Dockry. Gratitude to Chuck Schwab for my years of leadership opportunities there, with some of which I did well and others I did not—all of which readied me to help others. Thank you to Dick Boyatzi, Winn Hackett, and George Waal, who rode his Harley into the clouds way too soon, for their investment and belief in me during my years at PriceWaterhouse Consulting in Boston.

Thanks to Bill W. and Dr. Bob for the steps and traditions. They are the best kind of leaders around—the kind that change millions of lives for the better, even after they are gone. Their principles guided me in developing many of the practices here.

Thank you to Maury Polk and family for being in my life. Thanks to Joe Farris; Gale St. John; Bob Anderson; Jonathan Hulsh; Diana Bryant; Jan Hier-King; Myra Rothfield; David Magill; Susi Nittler, who left too soon; Linda Tarnay; Alex Shula; Gregory Rutchik; Ed Mercier; Angela Tomlinson; Denver Clearing; SPTI in Raleigh; Pam Tweedy; Roberto Alves De Lima; Suzanne Gaynor; Jonathan Warmund; Elinor MacKinnon; Steve Pascucci; Danny Field; members of the 2006-2007 Central Office Committee, Bill Torchiana; Heather Cowan; Theresa Johnson, Sheila Purnell, Harriette Harrington, the Lenscrafters RVP team, and the entire Luxottica organization; Jackie Barnes—nurse of the century (or two); Roger White; Leni Miller; Dr. Sherron Kell for her marketing advice; and Drew Suss—to name a few friends, teachers, and supporters, past and present.

Thanks also to Harvey for the extra wakeup call in February 2006.

Finally, to family: to Ray—partner, friend, confidante, tenacious Irish guy, and patient hero—you have my deepest love and gratitude—I'm the lucky one. To Agnes for her annoying yet loving ways, to Layla for her wonders, and to my in laws, Jenny, Josie, Pierre (and Helga and Pedro)—I'm grateful to be part of your wonderful family! Thanks to Nancy Peck, for her input on this book, and for being a pal, a guide, a coach, and an overall Top Mom. Thanks to my Father, Bill Peck for teaching me many lessons about leadership, and for his feedback as well. Thanks also to Bob Feldman, for being a father to me too. My love and gratitude to Ron Neiport, for years of support, friendship, and just being a miracle man. My love and thanks goes also to Coy Dugger for his enduring friendship and support. My thanks and love to my brother Ned Peck and sister Kate Nelson, for teaching me so much, and to Kate's family, Pat Peck, Maggie and family, Tim and Andrea and the girls; Beth; Andrea; Joe and Joey; my other sister Kate; and all other beings with them, great and small.

Author's Biography

David Peck is the founder and president of Leadership Unleashed (www.leadershipunleashed.com), an executive coaching and management consulting firm based in Palm Springs, California. His prior leadership experience includes a number of executive management positions: including at Charles Schwab & Company, Inc., where he built and ran several organizations as a Chief Operating Officer and Senior Vice President, including a new division he started, led, and developed into a $21 billion in client assets in three years, as a principal at Price Waterhouse Consulting, and in the not-for-profit world. Currently he writes the blog The Recovering Leader (www.recoveringleader.com), which includes hundreds of postings of interest to leaders. He began his business career in the mailroom of a bank in Waltham, Massachusetts, prior to which he was a professional modern dancer who worked with major choreographers in the field.

ISBN 142515325-9